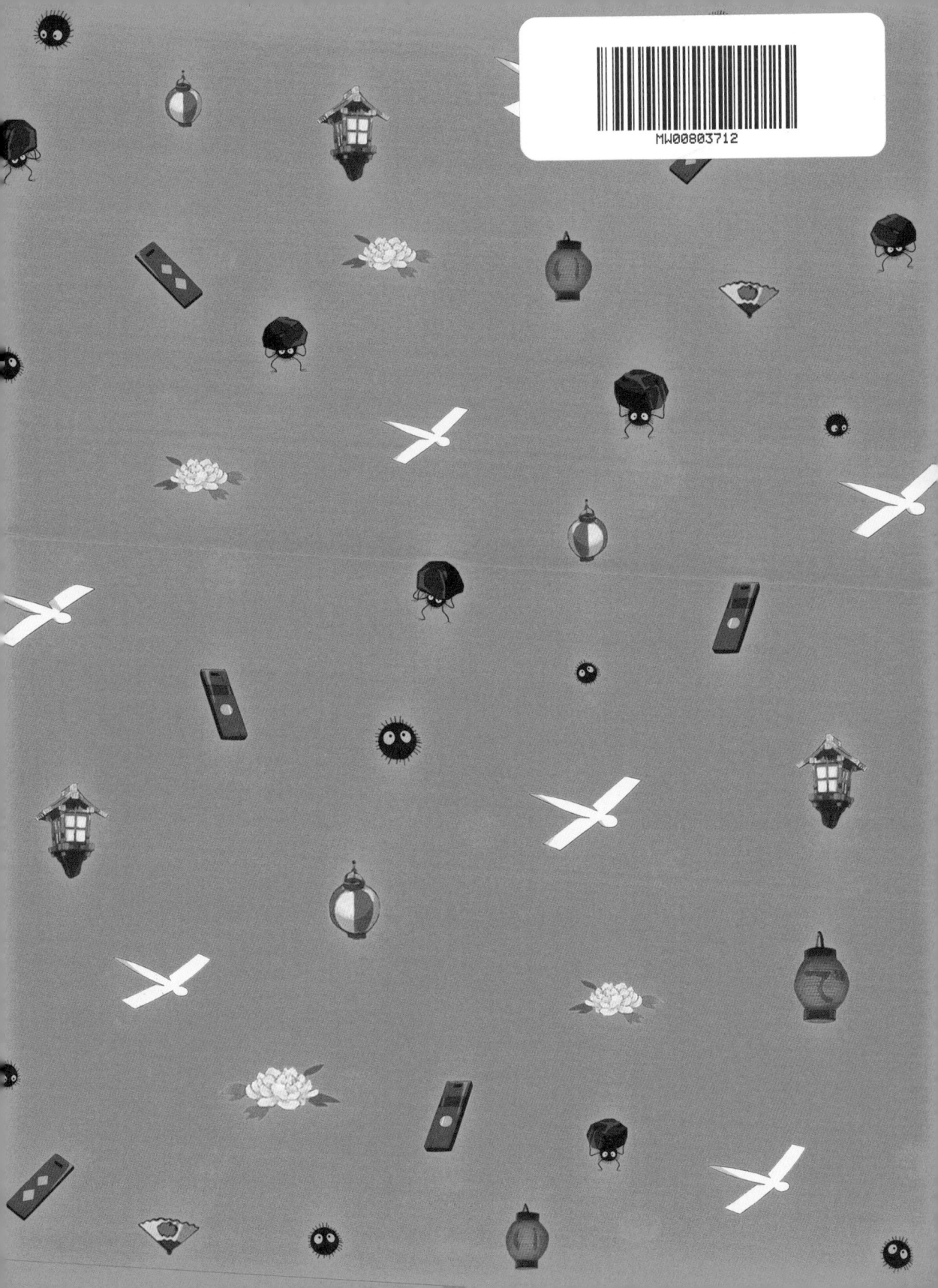

スタジオジブリ
STUDIO GHIBLI

Studio Ghibli is a Tokyo-based animation film studio
founded in 1985 by directors Isao Takahata and Hayao
Miyazaki. The studio has produced more than twenty
feature-length films, many of which have garnered numerous
awards and critical acclaim, including *My Neighbor Totoro*,
Kiki's Delivery Service, *Princess Mononoke*, and the Academy
Award-winning *Spirited Away*. Their last four films—*The Wind
Rises*, *The Tale of the Princess Kaguya*, *When Marnie Was
There*, and *The Red Turtle*—were all nominated for Academy
Awards for Best Animated Feature Film.

ISBN: 978-1-7972-0427-7

MIX
Paper from
responsible sources
FSC
www.fsc.org
FSC™ C169962

Manufactured in China.

10 9 8 7 6 5 4 3

CHRONICLE BOOKS
680 SECOND STREET
SAN FRANCISCO, CA 94107
WWW.CHRONICLEBOOKS.COM